LINKS
THE L
THE DEAD

TRANSFORMATION OF
EARTHLY FORCES
INTO CLAIRVOYANCE

RUDOLF STEINER

*Two lectures given to members of the
Anthroposophical Society in Bergen,
10th and 11th October, 1913*

Translated by D. S. Osmond and C. Davy

Rudolf Steiner Press
London

First edition (Anthroposophical Publishing Co) 1960
Second edition 1973

Translated from shorthand reports unrevised by the lecturer.
The original texts are included as the last two lectures in the
volume of the complete edition in German of the works of
Rudolf Steiner entitled: *Okkulte Untersuchungen über das
Leben zwischen Tod und neuer Geburt* (Bibl. Nr. 140).
This English edition is published by permission of the
Rudolf Steiner-Nachlassverwaltung, Dornach, Switzerland.

ISBN 0 85440 273 X

MADE AND PRINTED IN GREAT BRITAIN BY
THE GARDEN CITY PRESS LIMITED
LETCHWORTH, HERTFORDSHIRE
SG6 1JS

In his autobiography, *The Course of My Life* (chapters 35 and 36), Rudolf Steiner speaks as follows concerning the character and records of lectures and addresses printed originally for private circulation:

'The contents of this printed matter were intended as oral communications and not for print . . .

'They contain nothing that is not a pure expression of anthroposophical knowledge in its progressive development and growth . . . the reader may confidently take them as representing what Anthroposophy has to tell. Therefore it was possible, and moreover without misgivings . . . to depart from the accepted custom of circulating these publications only among the membership. But it will have to be remembered that faulty passages occur in the transcripts, which I myself did not revise.

'It is only reasonable to expect that anyone professing to pass judgment on the contents of this privately printed matter will be acquainted with the premises that were taken for granted when the words were spoken. These premises include, at the very least, the anthroposophical knowledge of Man and of the Cosmos in its spiritual essence; also what may be called "anthroposophical history", told as an outcome of research into the spiritual world.'

SUMMARY OF CONTENTS

5

form of clairvoyance will be the result, and under their influence there may be moral deterioration.

Transformation of the forces left over from the process of *learning to walk* and to *stand upright* leads to clairvoyant vision of life in the spiritual world preceding birth. These are the most innocent of all the forces in man's nature. In the aura around a tiny child, clairvoyance perceives these forces which still send their radiance into the life before birth.

The kind of clairvoyance needed for insight into the conditions of planetary existence described in the book *Occult Science* is developed from forces economized from those which have worked at the elaboration of the *grey matter of the brain*.

Souls in the spiritual world after the middle point of life between death and rebirth has been passed, direct their attention to the earth, and very diverse impressions come to such souls from what living human beings are thinking and feeling.

Anthroposophy is a sheer necessity for the earthly life of humanity and will become increasingly so in the immediate future .. 35
Bergen 11th October, 1913

I

LINKS BETWEEN THE LIVING AND THE DEAD

With all my heart I reciprocate the greeting of
your Chairman, and I am sure that those who
have come here with me to be together with
friends in Bergen will cordially join me in this.
It has been a beautiful journey through
mountains that were so welcoming and so
majestic, and I believe that everyone will be
happy during their stay in this old Hanseatic
city. A marvellous handiwork of man—the
railway by which we travelled—has given us
an impression seldom occurring in other
regions of Europe, an impression of human
creative power applied to Nature in her pure,
original state. When one sees rocks that had to
be shattered to pieces in order to produce a
work like this, and sees them lying side by side
with others piled up by Nature herself, impressions pour in which make a journey to a
country such as this one of the grandest that
can be undertaken nowadays. In this old city,
friends will spend happy days and keep them

7

in special remembrance because of their majestic background. These days will be enshrined in the memory especially because outer, physical evidence itself shows that, in this land too, anthroposophical hearts are beating in unison with our own pursuit of the spiritual treasures of humanity. It is quite certain that the visitors to this city will feel an even closer link of affection with those who have given us such a kindly reception.

*   *   *

As we are together here for the first time, I want to speak in an aphoristic way of matters pertaining to the spiritual world. Such matters are better and more easily expressed by word of mouth than in writing. This is not only because the prejudices existing in the world make it difficult in many respects to commit to writing everything that one so gladly conveys to *hearts* devoted to Anthroposophy, but it is also difficult because spiritual truths lend themselves better to the spoken word than to writing or to print.

This applies very specially to spiritual truths of a more intimate kind. For these things to be written down and printed always goes rather against the grain, although in our day it has to be done. It is always difficult to allow the more intimate truths relating to the higher worlds themselves to be written down and printed, precisely because writing and printing cannot be read by the spiritual Beings of whom one is speaking. Books cannot be read in the spiritual world.

True, for a short period after death books can still be read through remembrance, but the Beings of the higher Hierarchies cannot read our books. And if you ask: Do these Beings then not want to learn how to read?—I must tell you that according to my experience they show no desire at present to do so because they find that the reading of what is produced on the earth is neither necessary nor useful to them.

The spiritual Beings begin to read only when human beings on the earth read books—that is to say, when what is contained in the books *comes to life in the thoughts of men.* Then the spiritual Beings read in these thoughts; but what is written or printed is like darkness for the Beings of the spiritual worlds. And so when something is committed to writing or to print, one has the feeling that communications are being made behind the back of the spiritual Beings. This is a feeling which a man of modern culture may not wholly share, but every true occultist will experience this feeling of distaste for writing and print.

When we penetrate into the spiritual worlds

9

with clairvoyant vision, we see it to be of particular importance that knowledge of the spiritual world shall spread more and more widely during the immediate future, because upon this spread of Spiritual Science will depend a great deal in respect of a change that is becoming increasingly necessary in man's life of soul. If with the eyes of spirit we look back over a period measured by centuries only, we find something that may greatly astonish those who have no knowledge of these things. It is that intercourse between the living and the dead has become more and more difficult, that even a comparatively short time ago this intercourse was far more active and alive.

When a Christian of the Middle Ages, or even a Christian of more recent centuries, turned his thoughts in prayer to the dead who had been related or known to him, his prayers and feelings bore him upward to the souls of the dead with much greater power than is the case today. For the souls of the dead to feel warmed by the breath of the love streaming from those who looked upwards or sent their thoughts upward to them in prayer, was far easier in the past than it is today—that is, if we allow external culture to be our only guide.

Again, the dead are cut off from the living more drastically in the present age than they were a comparatively short time ago, and this makes it more difficult for them to perceive what is astir in the souls of those left behind. This belongs to the evolution of humanity, but evolution must also lead to a rediscovery of this connection, this real intercourse between the living and the dead.

In earlier times the human soul was still able to maintain a real connection with the dead, even if it was no longer a fully conscious one, because for long now men have ceased to be clairvoyant. In even more ancient times the living were able to look upwards with clair-voyant vision to the dead and to follow the happenings of their life. Just as it was once natural for the soul to be in living relationship with the dead, so it is possible today for the soul to re-establish this intercourse and relation-ship by acquiring thoughts and ideas about the spiritual worlds. And it will be one of the practical tasks of anthroposophical life to en-sure that the bridge is built between the living and the dead.

In order that we may really understand one another, I want to speak first of certain aspects of the mutual relationship between the living and the dead, starting with a quite simple phenomenon which will be explained in accord-ance with the findings of spiritual investiga-tions. Souls who sometimes practise a little self-contemplation will be able to observe the following (and I believe that many have done so). Let us suppose that someone has hated another person in life, or perhaps it was, or is, merely a question of antipathy or dislike. When the person towards whom hatred or antipathy was directed dies, and the other hears of his death, he will feel that the same hatred or antipathy cannot be maintained. If the hatred persists beyond the grave, sensitive souls will feel a kind of shame that it should be so. This feeling—and it is present in many souls—can be observed by clairvoyance. During self-examination the question may well be asked: Why is it that this feeling of shame at some hatred or antipathy arises in the soul, for the existence of such hatred was never at any time admitted to a second person?

When the clairvoyant investigator follows in the spiritual worlds the one who has passed through the gate of death and then looks back upon the soul who has remained on the earth, he finds that, generally speaking, the soul of the dead has a very clear perception, a very definite feeling, of the hatred in the soul of the living man. The dead sees the hatred—if I may speak figuratively. The clairvoyant investigator is able to confirm with all certainty that this is so. But he can also perceive what such hatred signifies for the dead. It signifies an obstacle to the good endeavours of the dead in his spiritual develop-

12

ment, an obstacle comparable with hindrances standing in the way of some external goal on earth. In the spiritual world the dead finds that the hatred is an obstacle to his good endeavours. And now we understand why hatred —even if there was justification for it in life— dies in the soul of one who practises a little self-contemplation: the hatred dies because a feeling of shame arises in the soul when the one who was hated has died. True, if the man is not clairvoyant he does not know the reason for this, but implanted in the very soul there is a feeling of being observed; the man feels: the dead sees my hatred and it is an actual hindrance to his good endeavours.

Many feelings rooted deeply in the human soul are explained when we rise into the worlds of spirit and recognize the spiritual facts underlying these feelings. Just as when doing certain things on earth we prefer not to be physically observed and would refrain from doing them if we knew this was happening, so hatred does not persist after a person's death when we have the feeling that we ourselves are being observed by him. But the love or even the sympathy we extend to the dead eases his path, removes hindrances from him.

What I am now saying—that hatred creates hindrances in the spiritual world and love removes them—does not cut across karma.

After all, many things happen here on earth which we shall not attribute directly to karma. If we knock our foot against a stone, this must not always be attributed to karma—not, at any rate, to moral karma. In the same way it is not a violation of karma when the dead feels eased through the love streaming to him from the earth, or when he encounters hindrances to his good endeavours.

Something else that will make an even stronger appeal in connection with intercourse between the dead and the living is the fact that in a certain sense the souls of the dead too need nourishment; not, of course, the kind of nourishment required by human beings on the earth, but of the nature of spirit-and-soul. By way of comparison, just as we on the earth must have cornfields where the grain for our physical sustenance ripens, so must the souls of the dead have cornfields from which they can gather certain sustenance which they need during the time between death and a new birth. As the eye of clairvoyance follows the souls of the dead, the souls of sleeping human beings are seen to be cornfields for the dead. For one who has this experience in the spiritual world for the first time, it is not only surprising but deeply shattering to see how the souls living between death and a new birth hasten as it were to the souls of sleeping human beings, seeking for the thoughts and ideas which are in those souls; for these thoughts are food for the souls of the dead and they need this nourishment.

When we go to sleep at night, the ideas and thoughts which have passed through our consciousness in our waking hours begin to live, to be living beings. Then the souls of the dead draw near and share in these ideas, feeling nourished as they perceive them. When clairvoyant vision is directed to the dead who night after night make their way to the sleeping human beings left behind on earth—especially blood-relations but friends as well—seeking refreshment and nourishment from the thoughts and ideas that have been carried into sleep, it is a shattering experience to see that they often find nothing. For as regards the state of sleep there is a great difference between one kind of thought and another.

If throughout the day we are engrossed in thoughts connected with material life, if our mind is directed only to what is going on in the physical world and can be achieved there, if we have given no single thought to the spiritual worlds before passing into sleep but often bring ourselves into those worlds by means quite different from thoughts, then we have no nourishment to offer to the dead. I know towns in Europe where students induce sleepiness by drinking a lot of beer! The result is that they carry over thoughts which cannot live in the spiritual world. And then when the souls of the dead approach, they find barren fields; they fare as our physical body fares when famine prevails because our fields yield no crops. Especially at the present time much famine among souls can be observed in the spiritual worlds, for materialism is already very widespread. Many people regard it as childish to occupy themselves with thoughts about the spiritual world but thereby they deprive souls after death of needed nourishment.

In order that this may be rightly understood, it must be stated that nourishment after death can be drawn only from the ideas and thoughts of those with whom there was some connection during life; nourishment cannot be drawn from those with whom there was no connection at all. When we cultivate Anthroposophy today in order that there may again be in souls a spirit-uality which can be nourishment for the dead, we are not working only for the living, or merely in order to provide them with some kind of theoretical satisfaction, but we try to fill our hearts and souls with thoughts of the spiritual world because we know that the dead who were connected with us on earth must draw their nourishment from these thoughts. We feel ourselves to be workers not only for living human beings, but workers too in the

. .

sense that anthroposophical activity, the spread of anthroposophical life, is also of service to the spiritual worlds. In speaking to the living for their life by day, we promote ideas which, bringing satisfaction as they do in the life by night, are fruitful nourishment for the souls whose karma it was to die before us. And so we feel the urge not only to spread Anthroposophy by the ordinary means of communication, but deep down within us there is the longing to cultivate Anthroposophy in communities, in groups, because this is of real value.

As I have said, the dead can draw nourishment only from souls with whom they were associated in life. We therefore try to bring souls together in order that the harvest-fields for the dead may become more and more extensive. Many a human being who after death finds no harvest-field because all his family are materialists, finds it among the souls of anthroposophists with whom he had had some connection. That is the deeper reason for working together in community, and why we are anxious that the dead should have been able before death to know anthroposophists who are still occupied on the earth with spiritual things; for when these people are asleep the dead can draw nourishment from them.

In ancient times, when a certain spirituality

17

pervaded the souls of men, it was among religious communities and blood-relatives that help was sought after death. But the power of blood-relationship has diminished and must be replaced by cultivation of the spiritual life, as is our endeavour. Anthroposophy can therefore promise that a new bridge will be built between the living and the dead and that through it we can mean something real to the dead. And when with clairvoyant vision today we sometimes find human beings in the life between death and a new birth suffering because they have known, including their nearest and dearest, harbour only materialistic thoughts, we recognize how necessary it is for cultural life on earth to be permeated with spiritual thoughts.

Suppose, for example, we find in the spiritual world a man who died fairly recently, whom we knew during his life on earth and who left behind certain members of his family also known to us. The wife and children were all of them good people in the ordinary sense, with a genuine love for one another. But clairvoyant vision now reveals that the father, whose wife was the very sun of his existence when he came home after heavy and arduous work, cannot see into her soul because she has not spiritual thoughts either in her head or in her heart. And so he asks: Where is my wife?

What has become of her? He can look back only to the time when he was united with her on earth, but now, when he is seeking her most urgently of all, he cannot find her. This may well happen. There are many people today who believe that as far as consciousness is concerned the dead have passed into a kind of void, who can think of the dead only with materialistic thoughts, not with any fruitful thoughts. In the life between death and rebirth a soul may be looking towards someone still on earth, someone who had loved him, but the love is not combined with belief in the soul's continued existence after death. In such a case, at the very moment after death when this desire arises to see one who was loved on earth, all vision may be extinguished. The living human being cannot be found, nor can any link be established with him, although it is known that he could indeed be contacted if spiritual thoughts were harboured in his soul.

This is a frequent and sorrowful experience for the dead. And so it may happen—this can be seen by clairvoyant vision—that many a human being after death encounters obstacles in the way of his highest aims on account of the thoughts of antipathy by which he is followed, and he finds no consolation in the living thoughts of those to whom he was dear on earth because owing to their materialism they are hidden from his sight.

The laws of the spiritual world, perceived in this way by clairvoyant vision, hold good unconditionally. That this is so is shown by an example which it has often been possible to observe. It is instructive to see how thoughts of hatred, or at least antipathy, take effect even if they are not conceived in full consciousness. There are school-teachers of the type usually known as 'strict', who are unable to gain the affection of their pupils; in such cases of course, the thoughts of antipathy and hatred are formed half innocently. But when such a teacher dies it can be seen how these thoughts too—for they persist—are obstacles in the way of his good endeavours in the spiritual world. After the teacher's death it is not often that a child or young person realizes that his hatred ought to cease, but he nevertheless preserves the feeling of how the teacher tormented him. From such insights a great deal can be learnt about the mutual relationships between the living and the dead.

I have been trying to lead up to something that can become a fundamentally good result of anthroposophical endeavour—namely, *reading to the dead*. It has been proved in our own Movement that very great service can be rendered to the souls of those who have died before us by reading to them about spiritual things. This can be done by directing your thoughts to the dead and, in order to make this easier, you can picture him as you knew him in life, standing or sitting before you. In this way you can read to more than one soul at a time. You do not read aloud, but you follow the ideas with alert attention, always keeping in mind the thought: The dead are standing before me.

That is what is meant by reading to the dead. It is not always essential to have a book, but you must not think abstractly and you must think each thought to the end. In this way you are able to read to the dead.

Although it is more difficult, this can be carried so far that if in the realm of some particular world-conception—or indeed in any domain of life—thoughts have been held in common with the soul of the dead and there has been some degree of personal relationship, one can even read to a soul with whom the connection has been no closer than this. Through the warmth of the thoughts directed to him, he gradually becomes attentive. Thus it may be of real use to read to distant associates after their death.

The reading can take place at any time. I have been asked what is the best hour of the day for such reading, but it is quite independent of time. All that matters is to think the thoughts through to the end; to skim through them is not enough. The subject-matter must be worked through word by word, as if one were reciting inwardly. Then the dead read with us. Nor is it correct to think that such reading can be useful only to those who have come into contact with Anthroposophy during their lifetime. This is by no means necessarily so.

Quite recently, perhaps not even a year ago, one of our friends, and his wife too, felt a kind of uneasiness every night. As the friend's father had died a short time previously, it struck him at once that his father was wanting something and was turning to him. And when this friend came to me for advice, it was found that the father, who during his lifetime would not listen to a word about Anthroposophy, was feeling an urgent need after his death to know something of it. Then, when the son and his wife read to the father the lecture-course on the Gospel of St. John which I once gave in Cassel, this soul felt deeply satisfied, as though lifted above many disharmonies that had been experienced shortly after death.

This case is noteworthy because the soul concerned was that of a preacher who had regularly presented the views of his religion to other men, but after death could only find satisfaction by being able to share in the reading of an anthroposophical elucidation of the Gospel of St. John. It is not essential that the one whom we wish to help after death should have been an anthroposophist in his lifetime, although in the nature of things very special service will be rendered to an anthroposophist by reading to him.

A fact such as this gives us a view of the human soul quite different from the one usually held. There are factors in the souls of men of far greater complexity than is generally believed. What takes its course consciously is actually only a small part of man's life of soul. In the unconscious depths of his soul there is a great deal going on of which he has at most a dim inkling; it hardly enters at all into his clear waking consciousness. Moreover, the very opposite of what a man believes or thinks in his upper consciousness may often be astir in his subconscious life. A very frequent case is that one member of a family comes to Anthroposophy and the brother or the husband or the wife become more and more hostile to it, often scornful and rabidly opposed. Great antipathy to Anthroposophy then develops in such a family and life becomes very difficult for many people because of the scorn and even anger of friends or relatives.

Investigation of these latter souls often reveals that in their subconscious depths an intense longing for Anthroposophy is developing. Such a soul may be longing for Anthroposophy even more intensely than someone who in his upper consciousness is an avid attender of anthroposophical meetings. But death lifts away the veils from the subconscious and balances out such things in a remarkable way. It often happens in life that a man deadens himself to what lies in the subconscious; there are people who may have an intense longing for Anthroposophy—but they deaden it. By raging against Anthroposophy they deaden this longing and delude themselves by repudiating it. But after death the longing asserts itself all the more forcibly. The most ardent longing for Anthroposophy often shows itself after death in the very people who have raged against it in life. Do not, therefore, refrain from reading to those who were hostile to Anthroposophy while they were alive, for by this reading you may often be rendering them the greatest service imaginable.

A question often raised in connection with this is: 'How can one be sure that the soul of the dead person is able to listen?' Admittedly, without clairvoyance it is difficult to be sure of this, although one who steeps himself in thoughts of the dead will in time be surprised by a feeling that the dead person is actually listening. This feeling will be absent only if he is inattentive and fails to notice the peculiar warmth that often arises during the reading. Such a feeling can indeed be acquired, but even if this proves not to be possible it must nevertheless be said that in our attitude to the spiritual world a certain principle always applies. The principle is that when we read to one who has died, we help him under all circumstances, if he hears us. Even if he does not hear us, we are fulfilling our duty and may eventually succeed in enabling him to hear. In any case we gain something by absorbing thoughts and ideas which will quite certainly be nourishment for the dead in the way indicated. Therefore under no circumstances is anything lost. Actual experience has shown that in fact this awareness of what is being read is extraordinarily widespread among the dead, and that tremendous service can be rendered to those to whom we read the spiritual wisdom that can be imparted to us today.

Thus we may hope that the wall dividing the living from the dead will become thinner and thinner as Anthroposophy spreads through the world. And it will be a beautiful and splendid result of Anthroposophy if in a future time men come to know—but as actual fact, not in theory only—that in reality it is only a matter of a transformation of experience when we ourselves have passed through so-called death and are together with the dead. We can actually enable them to share in what we ourselves experienced during physical life. A false idea of the life between death and rebirth would be indicated if the question were asked: 'Why is it necessary to read to the dead? Do they not know through their own vision what those on earth can read to them, do they themselves not know it far better?' This question will of course be asked only by one who is not in a position to know what can be experienced in the spiritual world. After all, we can live in the physical world without acquiring knowledge of it. If we are not in a position to form judgments about certain things, we have no real knowledge of the physical world. The animals live together with us in the physical world, but do not know it as we ourselves know it. The fact that a soul after death is living in the spiritual world does not mean that this soul has knowledge of that world, although he is able to behold it. The knowledge acquired through Anthroposophy can be acquired only on the earth; it cannot be acquired in the spiritual world. If, therefore, beings in the spiritual world are to possess knowledge, it must be learnt through those who themselves acquire it on earth. It is an important secret of the spiritual worlds that the soul can be in them and behold them, but that knowledge of them must be acquired on the earth.

At this point I must mention a common misconception about the spiritual worlds. When a human being is living in the spiritual world between death and a new birth, he directs his longing to our physical world somewhat as a physical human being directs his longing to the spiritual world. A man between death and a new birth expects from men on the earth that they will show and radiate up to him knowledge that can be acquired only on the earth. The earth has not been established without purpose in spiritual world-existence; the earth has been summoned to life in order that there may come into being that which is possible nowhere else. Knowledge of the spiritual worlds—which means more than vision, more than a mere onlooking—can arise only on the earth.

I said before that the beings of the spiritual worlds cannot read our books, and I must now add that what lives in us as Anthroposophy is for the spiritual beings, and also for our own souls after death, what books here on earth are for physical man—something through which he acquires knowledge of the world. But these books which we ourselves are for the dead, are *living* books. Try to feel the importance of these words: we must provide reading for the dead!

In a certain sense our books are more long-suffering, for they do not allow their letters to vanish away into the paper while we are reading them, whereas by filling our minds with material thoughts which are invisible in the spiritual worlds, we men often deprive the dead of the opportunity of reading. I am obliged to say this because the question is often raised as to whether the dead themselves are not capable of knowing what we are able to give them. They cannot be, because Anthroposophy can be grounded only on the earth and must be carried up from there into the spiritual worlds.

When we ourselves penetrate into the spiritual worlds and come to know something about the life there, we encounter conditions altogether different from those prevailing in physical life on earth. That is why it is so very difficult to describe these conditions in terms of human words and human thoughts. Any attempt to speak concretely about them often seems paradoxical.

To take one example only, I am able to tell you of a human soul after death together with whom it was possible—because of his special knowledge—to make certain discoveries in the spiritual world about the great painter

Leonardo da Vinci, particularly about his famous picture of the Last Supper, in Milan. When one investigates a spiritual fact in association with such a soul, this soul is able to indicate many things which ordinary clairvoyance might not otherwise have found in the Akasha Chronicle. The soul in the spiritual world is able to point them out, but can do so only if there is some understanding of what this soul is trying to convey. Something very noteworthy then comes to light.

Suppose that in company with such a soul one is investigating how Leonardo da Vinci created his famous picture. Today the picture is hardly more than a few patches of colour. But in the Akasha Chronicle one can watch Leonardo as he painted, one can see what the picture was once like—although this is not an easy thing to do. When the investigation is carried on in company with a soul who is not incarnate but has some connection with Leonardo da Vinci and his painting, one perceives that this soul is showing one certain things—for example, the faces of Christ and of Judas as they actually were in the picture. But one perceives, too, that the soul could not reveal this unless at the moment when it is being revealed there is understanding in the soul of the living investigator. This is a *sine qua non*. And only at the moment when the

soul of the living investigator is receptive to
what is being disclosed does the discarnate
soul itself learn to understand what is otherwise merely vision. To speak figuratively.—
After something has been experienced together
with such a soul—something that can be experienced only in the way described—this soul
says to one: You have brought me to the
picture and I feel the urge to look at it with
you. (The soul of the dead says this to the
living investigator because of the latter's desire
to investigate the picture.) Numerous experiences then arise. But a moment comes when the
discarnate soul is either suddenly absent or says
that it must depart. In the case of which I have
just told you, the discarnate soul said: Up to
now the soul of Leonardo da Vinci regarded
with approval what was being done, but does
not now desire the investigation to continue.

My object in telling you this is to describe
an important feature of the spiritual life. Just
as in physical life we know that we are looking
at this or that object—we see a rose, or whatever it may be—so in the spiritual life we
know: this or that being is seeing us, watching
us. In the spiritual worlds we have the constant
feeling that beings are looking at us. Whereas
in the physical world we are conscious that we
are observing the world, in the spiritual world
the experience is that we ourselves are being

observed, now from this side, now from that. We feel that eyes are upon us all the time, but eyes that also impel us to take decisions. With the knowledge that we are or are not being watched by eyes in favour of what we ought or ought not to do, we either do it or refrain. Just as we reach out to pick a flower that delights us because we have seen it, in the spiritual world we do something because a being there views it favourably, or we refrain from the action because we cannot endure the look that is directed at it. This experience must become ingrained in us. In the spiritual world we feel that we ourselves are being seen, just as here in the physical world we feel that we ourselves are seeing. In a certain sense, what is active here is passive in that other world, and what is active there is passive here.

From this it is obvious that quite different concepts must be acquired in order to understand correctly descriptions of conditions in the spiritual world. You will therefore realize how difficult it is to coin in words of ordinary human language descriptions of the spiritual world that one would so gladly give. And you will realize too how essential it is that for many things the necessary preparatory understanding shall first have been created.

There is only one other matter to which I want to call attention. The question may arise:

Why does anthroposophical literature describe in such a general sense what happens directly after death, in Kamaloca and in the realm of spirits (Devachan) and why is so little said about individual examples of clairvoyant vision? For it may well be believed that to observe a particular soul after death would be easier than to describe general conditions. But it is not so. I will use a comparison to explain this.

It is easier for rightly developed clairvoyance to survey the broad, general conditions—such as the passage of the human soul through death, through Kamaloca and upwards into Devachan than to perceive some particular experience of an individual soul. In the physical world it is easier to have knowledge of phenomena that are subject to the influences of the great movements of the celestial bodies and more difficult in the case of irregular phenomena caused by those movements. Every one of you will be able to predict that the sun will rise tomorrow morning and set in the evening; but it is not so easy to know exactly what the weather will be. The same holds good for clairvoyance. The knowledge of conditions usually portrayed in the descriptions of the spiritual worlds—conditions which are first perceived in clairvoyant consciousness—is to be compared with the knowledge of the general course taken by the heavenly bodies. And one can always count upon the fact that the data of such knowledge will generally prove correct.

Particular happenings in the life between death and rebirth are like the weather conditions here on the earth—which are, of course, also subject to law, but difficult to know with certainty. At one place one cannot be sure what kind of weather there is at another. Here in Bergen it is difficult to know what the weather is in Berlin, but not the positions of the sun or the moon. A special development of the faculty of clairvoyance is required to follow the course of an individual life after death, for to do this is more difficult than to follow the general course taken by the human soul.

On the right path, knowledge of the general conditions is acquired first, and only at the very end—if the necessary development has been achieved through training—knowledge of what would seem to be the easier. A man may have been able for some time to see conditions in Kamaloca or Devachan quite correctly and yet find it extremely difficult to see what time it is on the watch on his pocket. Things in the physical world present the greatest difficulty of all to clairvoyance.

In acquiring knowledge of the higher worlds it is exactly the opposite. Errors occur

33

here because a certain natural clairvoyance still exists; this clairvoyance is unreliable and prone to all kinds of aberrations, but it may long have been present without its possessor having clairvoyant sight of the general conditions described in Anthroposophy, which are easier for the trained clairvoyant.

This is what I wanted to say to you today about the spiritual worlds. In the lecture tomorrow we will continue and to some extent deepen these studies.

II

THE TRANSFORMATION OF EARTHLY FORCES INTO CLAIRVOYANT FACULTIES

During the process of acquiring anthroposophical knowledge many questions may be asked on different points. Such questions are fully justified and we will devote part of our study today to the consideration of them. The answers will often lead more deeply into the whole complex of cosmic facts in so far as the spiritual world plays into them, and especially into the complex of facts connected with man's nature itself.

A person who has gradually come to realize the far-reaching significance of reincarnation may ask: Why is it that in ordinary life today man cannot become conscious of earlier earth-lives? Clairvoyant consciousness is able as it were so to extend the memory that earlier lives on earth rise up as remembrances, but in normal present-day humanity this does not happen.

35

From the standpoint of clairvoyant investigation the question takes the following form. It is clear, of course, that the faculty needed for clairvoyant investigation arises from within man himself, his own soul. He transcends the level of the ordinary human standpoint and reaches that of clairvoyance; hence the forces which subsequently make it possible to look back to previous earth-lives must be present in every human being. And now the question is: What happens to these forces, what does human nature do with these forces which, although they are present in a man, are born with him, he does not develop to the point where they enable him to remember earlier lives on earth?

When this question and the forces relevant to it are investigated by clairvoyance, observation must be directed to a very early age of childhood. For it is only then that the forces which can be used for retrospective clairvoyant vision into earlier earth-lives are to be seen at work. In present-day humanity these forces are used for the development of the larynx and everything connected with its functions. They are used especially for the development of that which later on makes the human larynx capable of *learning to speak*. Therefore the forces that would enable a man to look back into earlier incarnations are there in everyone; but in the present age they are used to such an extent for the development of the *organs of speech* that in normal circumstances this remembrance of the past is beyond man's reach.

There were, of course, epochs when nearly all over the earth men had this faculty of remembrance. The explanation is that retrospective vision into earlier earth-lives is not deprived of *all* the forces used for the development of the speech-organs; even while these organs are being formed, certain forces are kept back. In the process of evolution, speech has gradually assumed a form which in the present cycle of time summons up many more forces—especially of the etheric body—than it did in earlier epochs. Hence the forces that remain after the greater part of them have been applied in forming the larynx are left entirely unused by modern man. Were he to take account of them—as the clairvoyant must do—he would be able to look back into earlier earth-lives.

I indicated in the public lecture here* that that if a man succeeds in developing the activity of the etheric body that is otherwise unfolded only in exercising the organs of speech, if he succeeds in releasing the forces from these organs, in being able as it were to listen inwardly without speaking aloud and in intensifying this experience, then the exercise of these

* *Riddles of Life.* 9.X.13.

forces is actually able to call forth the memory of earlier lives on earth. A man of the present pays no attention to the forces of speech which remain unused and can be applied for looking back into earlier incarnations. This is a case where clairvoyant investigation can indicate the origin of the forces in normal life which would otherwise enable men to have insight into the spiritual life.

The same applies to the forces which in the human being of today are used to bring into being the so-called *grey matter of the brain*—the main organ of thinking. Thinking is not, of course, actually engendered by the brain, but in order to think the brain is needed as an instrument. The *forces of thinking* which, if they were all at man's disposal, would enable him easily to grasp what is contained, for example, in my book *Occult Science*, are used in the case of the normal human being today to organize and co-ordinate the grey substance of the brain.

The high degree of co-ordination in the brain-substance of the average man nowadays was not present in the men of ancient Greece, about the sixth or fifth century B.C. Human nature changes in this respect more rapidly than is supposed. In the Greeks of the pre-historic epoch—the tenth, eleventh, twelfth centuries B.C.—there arose quite naturally at a certain age the clairvoyance that can now again be given expression as Spiritual Science. And the forces which to this day remain over from the elaboration of the grey substance of the brain must be exercised in the way described in order to survey with clarity and definition what is presented in my book *Occult Science*.

It is really not difficult, even for a modern man, to acquire the qualifications for describing the spiritual world. Indeed it might almost be said to be a matter of surprise that there are not numbers of people today with a quite natural vision of these conditions of existence —and it is also surprising that descriptions of them meet with such vehement antagonism. For it is not difficult, comparatively speaking, to attain the degree of clairvoyance necessary for vision of these things. All that need be done is the following—although in such matters the saying in *Faust* may well apply: 'True, 'tis easy, yet is the easy hard.'

The most vigorous development of the brain takes place during the first years of life; it is then that clairvoyance sees the etheric body, and the astral body too, working most actively of all at the moulding and articulation of the brain. But this work goes on for some considerable time. Although the process is slower in later years, it is no exaggeration to say that through what he learns from life man becomes cleverer and cleverer; elaboration of the grey matter of the brain does not cease. But the following principle is not noticed, nor can one really expect it to be. If in a certain year a man resolves to give up a favourite spiritual pursuit ... it would have to be one connected with external matters because it is through this kind of activity that the brain-substance is moulded, although Anthroposophy can of course be studied, provided it is not studied just like some other science ... if this man resolves to give up some favourite pursuit for seven years and strictly adheres to this, trying in silent meditation to awaken the forces which have been economized in this way but would have been used differently if the pursuit had continued, then it will be comparatively easy for him to acquire a high degree of knowledge at least of the conditions described in the book *Occult Science*. The fact that so few achieve this merely shows that very little is done in this direction. The effort is not carried through, because anyone who has a favourite pursuit will seldom have sufficient self-denial to abandon it entirely for seven whole years. So you see that part of the knowledge that can be given out today is within comparatively easy reach.

When you think of the amazing achievements of modern culture it will not surprise you that many forces of the etheric body are devoted to elaborating the brain, for this culture is almost entirely a product of the activity of the brain; the forces are all absorbed in this task. Someone might say: Yes, but I have taken no part whatever in creating this culture! Everyone can delude himself in this respect, but the facts remain. On the earth today there is scarcely a spot, however isolated, where outer culture does not penetrate to such an extent that man's thinking is engaged with it. And that in itself suffices to divert the forces from the attainment of clairvoyant consciousness.

True, it might be said that savages do not concern themselves with what is thus elaborated by the brain. But neither can it be said of savages today that they unfold any particular clairvoyant forces in this direction. This is because a definite spiritual law prevails, namely that there must be special preparation for what is thus to be acquired by means of clairvoyance. A savage might possibly be able to develop clairvoyant forces of a quite different kind, but not those required for vision of what is described in *Occult Science*, because he has undergone no preparation for it. These forces must be *the outcome of the transformation of other forces.*

Again, it might be argued: But a great many people have no pet occupation! Why is it that they have not become clairvoyant? The reason is that the development of the forces of clairvoyance does not originate from nothingness but from the transformation of what already exists. Forces must already have been developed in a certain direction; the preliminaries for the intelligence belonging to modern culture must already have been there. The exercise of these forces must be renounced for a time ... and then they are transformed. This is what enables the facts described in *Occult Science* to be followed clairvoyantly. Such descriptions are made possible by applying the forces which normally enable the brain to make use of the forces of intelligence in its higher form.

On the other hand, it is the transformation of different forces and faculties which leads, not to these wide, universal vistas, but to the discovery of particular conditions. For example, the faculty of looking back into earlier earth-lives is acquired by keeping back certain forces otherwise used entirely for the development of the organs of speech in the way described.

I have now spoken of two kinds of forces which enable man to have clairvoyant vision of the spiritual worlds. I have spoken of the forces used in the present age for the elaboration of the grey matter of the brain; the forces enabling man to look back to earlier lives on earth are connected with the development of speech. But there are still other forces which make it possible to see in greater detail what lies between death and a new birth and what is happening to an individual human being during that period of existence. It is the more general conditions that are described in *Occult Science*. But it is a different matter to see right into the spiritual world itself; other forces hardly noticed in life are required for that.

There is something that entails the exercise of a great many forces—the fact that man does not go about on all fours throughout his life but at an early age acquires the faculty of *standing upright*. The forces enabling man to assume the vertical position are of such a nature that they inspire a quite special reverence in one who has penetrated into the spiritual world. For a person capable of clairvoyant investigation a wonderful mystery is contained in the spectacle of a child learning to walk. Certain of the forces used by the human being in early childhood in order to stand upright, remain over, but they are taken all too little into account. These are the forces which make insight possible into the world where the life between death and a new birth is spent.

There are other ways of achieving this, but the following is one. When a man succeeds in

43

recollecting how he learnt to *walk* and the nature of the efforts made, he discovers in himself the forces that have been saved up in his etheric body, for it is the etheric body that must be specially exerted then. If he seeks out these forces—and they are present in every-one—he can summon from his own being much that enables him to look back into the life spent between death and rebirth.

You may ask: How can this be achieved? If we have the good fortune to be able to promulgate our Anthroposophical Movement ... well, it can be said that we have already made a beginning with the summoning of these forces. If things go well, they become active only after a period of seven years has passed —but a beginning has been made and this beginning will develop further in human nature. These forces that have been saved generally remain unheeded, but awareness of them can be promoted by practising a certain form of dance. This awareness can of course also be aroused through meditation ... but for a little less than a year now, certain groups of people among us have been working at Eurythmy,* an art based on the principles of the movements of the etheric body.

* See *Eurythmy as Visible Speech.* Fifteen lectures given in Dornach, June/July, 1924. (Anthroposophical Publishing Co., 1956.)

Eurythmy is nothing like ordinary gymnastics or dancing—which are really of little account—but the movements made are in complete accord with those of the etheric body. Through these free movements the human being will gradually discover and become aware of the forces that are still within him. Foundations are being created for the awakening of forces within the human being which will really enable him to see into the spiritual worlds stretching between his last death and his birth in the present life.

In these and other ways Anthroposophy can be a really practical factor in cultural life. And we may be sure that Anthroposophy will not stop at the teaching of truths in the abstract but man himself, in his whole being, will be affected in such a way that the awakening of forces now slumbering within him will lead to actual spiritual experience.

These things that have to be said here are strange, but they are realities. When a man discovers the forces that have remained over from the process of learning to walk, this enables him to see with clairvoyant vision the worlds in which he lives between death and a new birth. This can also be achieved through meditation, but meditation must then become *feeling*, and feeling is the most difficult experience of all to acquire through meditation.

It is therefore a matter of discovering the forces which enable man to see into the world stretching between death and rebirth, to see happenings that took place some long time before birth. In this realm there is a great deal that for the first time makes life really comprehensible. For example, some misfortune befalls us. To begin with, our one and only feeling is that it is indeed a misfortune. Did we but know why it was that decades, even centuries, before birth, we ourselves so arranged conditions that this misfortune should befall us, many things would be easier to bear! For then we should know that the misfortune is an ordeal, helping us to progress. Many other things, too, are experienced when we look into that realm of the spiritual world where the preparation for the present life has been undergone.

I will not now describe the general conditions, for that has been done in my writings. I will try to show by certain examples how the life before birth influences the life after birth. Strange as it may seem, when we have passed the middle point of life between death and rebirth—this life lasts for centuries, so there is naturally a middle point—the soul's attention in the spiritual world is directed mainly to the earth below. And after this middle point more and more impressions come to the soul from what is being done down there, from what human beings on earth are thinking and feeling; definite impressions are received by every individual soul.

For example, a soul may be passing into the second half of the spiritual life leading towards its new birth and may perceive more and more clearly those men who on the earth below are, let us say, pioneers of the coming epoch—men who are spiritually active. Certain individuals among these spiritually active men prove to be of great value to the soul. It even happens that the eyes of a soul are directed from the spiritual world very particularly to one or two figures on the earth.

Let us assume that a man born in the second half of the nineteenth century was in the spiritual world at the beginning of the nineteenth and during the second half of the eighteenth centuries. From that world the gaze of the soul is directed to men of significance in the cultural life of the time. Among them are certain individuals whom the soul particularly values and greatly loves. One of the experiences in that world is that souls look downwards to the human beings who are evolving on the earth. Moreover, these human beings on earth are influenced, although not in a way that encroaches upon freedom; the effect of the influence is that certain things arise more easily in the souls of these individuals on earth because some being is looking downwards to them from the spiritual world. Thus are men on earth stimulated to creative work and activity by souls who will be be born at a later time and whose gaze is directed to them from the spiritual world. This can happen in matters both of a general and of a more intimate kind.

The case has occurred of a soul living in the spiritual world during the eighteenth and first half of the nineteenth centuries; an outstanding personage on earth becomes this soul's ideal. One sees what the soul would fain become, how its desire is to find this personage after birth. For example, the soul sees the books of the man he desires to emulate. Thus the soul looks down from heaven to earth with a certain inner yearning, a certain inner urge, just as a living man—although with somewhat different feelings—looks upwards with longing to the Beyond, to the heavens. But there is this great difference: when a man on earth looks upwards to the heavens without any knowledge of Anthroposophy these heavens remain more or less undefined, indistinct. The human being who is living in the spiritual world, however, is able to see with great exactitude the conditions prevailing on the earth, the human souls there for whom he has particular admiration, whose writings he perhaps longs to read.

In short, during the second half of spiritual

existence between death and a new birth one learns to know the souls of men in detail, to look right into these souls. And we ourselves, living now, can be aware that yonder in the spiritual world there are souls waiting to be born in decades of the near future; they gaze into our souls with longing, seeing there what they need as preparation for their earthly existence. During the period of their spiritual life they see our souls with vision as distinct as earthly man's vision of his heaven is indistinct.

This again is an indication of the fact that even if we have only a little knowledge of the spiritual worlds, the feeling comes that we are being observed. And so indeed we are, in manifold ways. The eyes of beings in the spiritual worlds, especially of those for whom the time has come to be born, are directed to our souls. Here again is a proof that the influence of Anthroposophy cannot possibly be harmful, for it helps to make what a man has in his soul worthy of observation by souls as yet unborn.

Clairvoyant investigation of these things brings momentous, often shattering experiences. One profoundly moving experience is when we look up to souls in the spiritual worlds who are on the way to birth, and see how they are gazing down to the earth, seeking for those who might become their parents. In earlier

49

epochs this was of greater consequence than it is today. But even now it is still one of the most moving experiences to observe such souls, for infinitely diverse impressions are received. I will describe one such impression of something that may actually happen.

A soul about to incarnate knows, for example, that in the coming earthly life it will need a particular kind of education, that certain knowledge will have to be assimilated even in early youth. But now the soul realizes: either here or there it would be possible to acquire such knowledge. This, however, is possible only by renouncing parents who in another respect would have been able to ensure a happy existence and by resorting to parents who may be quite unable to do so. If other parents were chosen the soul would be forced to admit: In those circumstances what is most important of all will be beyond my reach.

It must not be imagined that *all* conditions of the spiritual life differ entirely from those on the earth. One sees souls who before birth are in the throes of fierce inner conflict. For example, one may see a soul who is realizing: In my youth I may be ill-treated by rough parents. When a soul is in this situation, the fierce inner conflict begins. Many souls in the spiritual world bring this conflict upon themselves while preparing for birth. It must here be said that these struggles constitute a kind of external world for the soul. What I am now describing is not an inner conflict only, not a conflict of the heart only, but it is projected outwards and is, so to speak, around the soul. One sees in all definition the Imaginations which show that these souls must go forward to their coming incarnation inwardly torn asunder.

When we think about these conditions, it will readily occur to us why so many people have an aversion to Anthroposophy. They would much prefer it to be true that after death man enters for all time into eternal bliss. But it is not so. Moreover, it is well that things are as they are, for under these conditions the world will eventually reach the degree of perfection destined for it.

Curiously enough, the capacity to see into one's own life or that of another in the spiritual world comes from the forces of the etheric body that have been saved over from the process of learning to walk. But seership shows that these forces, when they have really unfolded, are in a certain respect superior to the forces of clairvoyance developed with the object of looking back into earlier earth-lives. Please take particular notice of this difference, for it throws light on many things.

There is no easier way of unfolding a

dangerous form of clairvoyance than by the development of those forces which in modern man are there for the purpose of producing the organs of speech and which, if kept back, enable him to look into earlier incarnations; for these forces are connected most closely of all with the lower instincts and passions in man's nature. And by nothing is a man brought so near to Lucifer and Ahriman as by the development of these forces which, at a certain level, enable him to look back into his own earlier earth-lives or into those of others. They lead to illusions; but above all, if they are not rightly developed, they have the effect that under their influence the clairvoyant may deteriorate morally, rather than the reverse. So the very forces which make vision of earlier incarnations possible are the most dangerous of all. They should be unfolded only when at the same time a man pays full attention to the development of pure morality in his own being. Because morality in its purest form is essential if it is desired to unfold these forces, experienced teachers will not readily countenance any systematic development of the powers which enable man to look into earlier incarnations.

Moreover this can be said: It is as common to find a certain lower kind of clairvoyance which looks into other worlds and can give descriptions of spiritual regions, as it is rare to find evidence of the development of genuine, objective vision into earlier incarnations as the result of the exercise of the forces of speech alone. As a rule, therefore, recourse is had to yet other measures when it is desired to train the capacity to look back into earlier incarnations. And here we come to an interesting point, showing how necessary it is to pay attention to things of which otherwise little account is taken.

It will seldom happen that spiritual guidance brings a person to the point of being able, merely by the development of the forces of speech, to look back to earlier lives on earth. In the present age many individuals could be capable of this, but as a rule it is achieved by different means. One of these means will seem strange, although it is based on a profound truth.

Suppose someone lives intensely in his inner life. It would cost him excessive strain, or possibly lead to overpowering temptations, were he to succeed, merely by developing the forces of speech, to look back in the light of karma at his earlier incarnations. Hence the spiritual Powers have recourse to a different means. Apparently by chance, he meets someone who mentions a name or a particular epoch or people. This works upon his soul from

53

outside in such a way that the mental picture sets astir the forces which help to promote clairvoyance. And then he becomes aware that this name or reference—although the speaker himself knew nothing about it—is a pointer, helping him to look into earlier lives on earth. In such a case there has been recourse to an outer means. The man in question hears the name of a person or of an epoch or of a people and is thus stimulated from outside to look back into previous incarnations. Such stimuli are sometimes exceedingly important for clairvoyant contemplation of the world. An experience seems to have been quite accidental but it provides a stimulus for powers of clairvoyance that would otherwise have remained rudimentary.

These are aphoristic indications on the subject of the penetration of the spiritual world into our earthly world. Actually, of course, the process is highly complicated.

Looking back into earlier earth-lives is therefore connected with forces fraught with danger because they lead to deception, to delusion. On the other hand, hardly anyone who develops the forces of clairvoyance leading to insight into the life in the spirit preceding birth will be prone to misuse these forces. As a rule it will be souls of a certain purity, in whom there is a certain natural morality, who look back with reliable vision into the life in the spiritual world preceding the present life on earth. This is connected with the fact that the forces of clairvoyance used for looking into this particular period of existence are the forces of childhood, those that have been left over from the process of learning to walk. They are the most innocent of all the forces in man's nature.

I ask you to pay attention to this, for it is very significant: The most innocent forces are at the same time those which, when they are developed, enable man to look into the life preceding birth. That, too, is why there is such enchantment in the sight of a tiny child, for in the aura playing around it are the forces which still send their radiance into the life before birth. In the aura of a child whose very countenance bears the stamp of innocence and otherworldliness, clairvoyant contemplation may perceive something that is truly more interesting than what comes to expression in the aura of many a grown-up person. The conflicts that were passed through in the spirit-land before birth and have determined destiny make the aura round the child into something full of glory, full of wisdom. The wisdom manifesting in the aura of a child is often far greater than anything which at a later age he will be able to express in words. The physiognomy may still lack definition, but very much can be revealed to the clairvoyant when he is able to see what is playing around a child. And if the forces present in childhood are developed later on into clairvoyance, vision becomes possible of the actual conditions preceding birth by a considerable period.

To look into this world may not, perhaps, be gratifying to egoism but to one who wishes to understand the whole setting of world-existence this vista, too, is of absorbing interest. Investigation in the Akasha Chronicle concerning certain outstanding figures in world-history consists not only in trying to discover what kind of life they lived on the physical plane, but how, as souls in the spiritual world between death and rebirth, they made preparation for this life.

The forces which, if kept unsullied, shine into earlier incarnations are saved, not so much in childhood but in the period of life when passions, moreover often in their worst form, unfold in the human being. These forces, which of course have other functions as well in human nature, develop much later than those of speech. They have to do with the emotions of sensual love and everything connected with them. There is a direct relationship between the forces leading to sensual love and those leading to speech—in the male this comes to expression in the breaking of the voice. It is at this age in life that many of these forces are saved. If they are kept pure they lead to the retrospective vision of earlier lives on earth. If they are not kept pure, if they come to be associated with sensual instincts in man they may lead to the greatest occult abuses. The forces of clairvoyance which originate and are held back at this age in life are also those that are most easily subject to temptation. You will now be able to grasp the whole connection!

The seer who gladly speaks about the period stretching between death and rebirth—some of you will have noticed that in other circles this is seldom mentioned—such a seer has developed particularly the forces saved from very early childhood. But a clairvoyant who speaks a great deal—fallaciously for the most part—about the earlier incarnations of individuals, must be distrusted. Some cases occur very frequently, for many people come out with utterances about earlier incarnations as if they were handing them out on a tray! A clairvoyant of this type must be distrusted because in this domain it is all too easy to evoke the forces most liable to temptation. The forces that can be saved for this purpose are saved at the time of life when sensual love is developing, and before the human being has taken his place in the social life. At times these forces give rise to a great deal of malpractice, especially to a definite occult malpractice, because they, more than any others, contribute to the promotion of delusion after delusion in the domain of the spiritual world.

Why are the assertions of clairvoyants who are exposed to these temptations so often false? It is because when the forces saved from this age of life are put into application, the lower instincts and urges immediately rise out of the human being like mist. And then Ahriman and the Ahrimanic spirits approach and out of this rising mist create *ghosts, spectres,* which can be seen and taken to be earlier incarnations.

The kind of clairvoyance needed for descriptions such as are given in the book *Occult Science* will be developed particularly easily by saving forces which can be held back only at a later age. And because at this age—after the twenty-first until the twenty-eighth years—the human being is usually developing forces concerned more with the intellectual life, with the life that is associated with a certain element of dispassion, investigations in this domain are the least subject to error and delusion. Thus knowledge of the great spiritual conditions in world-existence is acquired through the development of the forces which work in man's being at the elaboration of the brain.

The spirit-region proper, the region that is of particular interest at the time when a new life is in preparation, can be investigated by means of the forces saved in earliest childhood, at the age when the human being is learning to walk.

Admittedly, these are astonishing facts, but if we desire to penetrate into the spiritual worlds we must accustom ourselves to assimilate many ideas which, to begin with, seem paradoxical. The spiritual world, however, is not a mere continuation of the physical world of sense; indeed in many respects it is in utter contrast to the physical world. Man is revealed to us as a being occupying a place of great significance in the universe when on the one side we consider his destiny, his faculties and abilities in his earthly life, and when on the other side—through knowledge of spiritual reality—we see how between death and a new birth he passes through phases of life altogether different from that of the earth. It is then that the true significance and destination of man are revealed to us.

In these two lectures I wanted to describe various matters relating to the spiritual world. I have thought it advisable to speak in a rather aphoristic way because it is the first time we have been together in this city, and most of you will already be familiar with the systematic presentations contained in the books and writings—and also because I wanted to give certain supplementary information. It seemed to me that this would be more useful to the friends here than if I had dealt with a more connected chapter of Anthroposophy.

One's wish—you will allow me to say this at the end of what has been, for me too, such a happy gathering—is that Anthroposophy may penetrate as deeply as possible into the hearts and souls of men at the present time! For two things are important. First, when we observe the life around us and the facts of that life, seeing that the greatest cultural achievements are having the effect of making men more and more materialistic . . . then we realize how increasingly necessary Anthroposophy is to humanity, how great is men's need of it for the very reason that external life makes them into materialists. Because the most brilliant achievements of external life have this effect, men need the counterweight provided by Anthroposophy. Anthroposophy is a necessity for the earthy life of humanity and will become increasingly so in the immediate future. And anyone who reflects that external life in materialism would be doomed to sterility and to gradual death, caused precisely by the highest achievements of culture, will have the intense longing that Anthroposophy may find its way into the hearts and souls of men.

Our culture will make greater and greater

progress; but true as it is that many birds of song disappear from areas where the chimneys of factories tower up, true as it is that they are driven away by the smoke pouring from these chimneys, it is equally true that although we need everything that culture can give us—railways, steamships, telephones, aircraft, and so on—although nothing is to be said against the progress of external culture, nevertheless happiness, vigour, harmony and vitality of the life of soul would inevitably wilt and die under the influence of material culture if Anthroposophy did not bring spirituality to the souls of men. Therefore anyone who has insight into existing conditions cannot but long most profoundly that Anthroposophy will spread—for it is a sheer necessity.

On the other side the fact must be faced that as a result of this materialistic culture men have never rejected, nay even hated, Anthroposophy as vehemently as they do today. And these two facts—*necessity* and *misunderstanding* confront us today like two pillars between which we must pass if a place is to be created in the world for Anthroposophy. For those of us who endeavour to prepare other souls for the assimilation of Anthroposophy, a challenge is inscribed on each of these pillars—an urgent challenge to do everything that brings ourselves and those who are willing for it to Anthroposophy.

It was from this standpoint that I wanted to speak to you during this, my first visit to this city. And I should like my words of farewell to be these: Would that something of what I have been able to say have passed into your hearts and feelings, not into your heads alone! Then you will feel even more deeply and fundamentally united with us and with all who would like to bear this Movement more widely into the world than they have done hitherto. Because up to now we could not be together in space and this has happened for the first time, it is the wish of all of us that this gathering will have strengthened and made closer the bond between our souls.

With this I take leave of you, my dear friends, and of this beautiful city, with the consciousness that when such a gathering has taken place, it becomes the stimulus for a communion not dependent upon space or time. Let my farewell to you be this: May it be that through being together in space the stimulus has been given for an unbroken and enduring communion in the spirit.

Brief list of relevant books and lectures by Rudolph Steiner

Theosophy. An Introduction to the Super-sensible Knowledge of the World and the Destination of Man
Occult Science—an Outline
 (notably Chapter III)
The Dead are With Us
Man's Life on Earth and in the Spiritual Worlds
Earthly Death and Cosmic Life
The Inner Nature of Man and the Life Between Death and Rebirth
Verses and Meditations (pp. 200 et seq. for meditations in relation to the Dead)

All the published works of Rudolf Steiner in print in English, as well as those by other authors on anthroposophical subjects, can be obtained through
Rudolph Steiner Press
35 Park Road, London NW1 6XT

COMPLETE EDITION

of the works of Rudolf Steiner in the original German. Published by the *Rudolf Steiner Nachlassverwaltung*, Dornach, Switzerland, by whom all rights are reserved.

General Plan (abbreviated):

A. WRITINGS

I. Works written between 1883 and 1925
II. Essays and articles written between 1882 and 1925
III. Letters, drafts, manuscripts, fragments, verses, inscriptions, meditative sayings, etc.

B. LECTURES

I. Public Lectures
II. Lectures to Members of the Anthroposophical Society
on general anthroposophical subjects
Lectures to Members on the history of the Anthroposo-
~~phical Movement and the~~ ~~~~anthroposophical Society~~

~~~~k:

Arts,

d,
at

s,

s,
A
1d

ss
er